IN MEMORY OF...
My mother and father, Myrtle and J. P. Karem

DEDICATION
To my five sons:

Jon
Steven
Daniel
Thomas
Andrew
They are my best friends.

SARAH
A Real Woman who believed that He who promised is faithful.

from Hebrews 11:11

ACKNOWLEDGEMENTS

These are the Real Women on my team.
I would not have finished this book without them.

THE SPECIAL TEAM

Ginny Brown who encouraged, typed, edited, and
helped me score the touchdown.

MOST VALUABLE PLAYERS

These women did not give up when the game got too rough.
They hung in there. They played fair and they went by the rules.
They set great examples. They are winners! Rita Ayres, Susan
Davis, Mary Ellen Hunt, Sandy Karem, Carol Osborne, Brenda
Connolly Palmer, and Ruth Stanton.

THE BACKUP QUARTERBACKS

The English Women - Kimberle, Dina, Kim and Michelle

...AND THE COACH
My husband Wally, without all his calls I couldn't
have had all this fun.

A special thanks to the OFFICIALS who tended the game clock and kept the book in play. My editor, Nancy Mortensen, who understood the game plan and made it work. The graphic designer, Dan Dena, who put the game plan together.

TABLE OF CONTENTS

WHO AM I TO TELL YOU?

Football practice started and the honeymoon was over. Married life was football life. I began my football education on our wedding day, and it has continued for more than 40 years. I should have known what life would be like married to a football coach when Wally was an hour late for our wedding because football practice was extra long. His excuse to me, my father, and the assembled invited guests was *football practice*. Little did I know this would be a phrase frequently heard in our home. Our whole wedding was planned around football practice, the date, the honeymoon, and even the return home. We had one week for our honeymoon because Wally had to report for his first coaching position eight days after the wedding. I know now that the word *honeymoon* was not in his football playbook. His game plan was executed around driving to Wisconsin to observe the Green Bay Packers' training camp, make notes, and prepare himself for his new job in Louisville, Kentucky.

Wally had gone to high school with Paul Hornung who won the Heisman Trophy at Notre Dame. Paul was playing with the Green Bay Packers. Vince Lombardi was the coach. At that time I didn't have any idea who Lombardi was.

We spent several days at the training camp. Here I was, this young bride, watching all these gorgeous men running up and down the field. It really was fun because I'd never seen such big guys, strong guys, powerful guys--so many men in one place. What a way to start a marriage!

I remember distinctly standing there on the sidelines when a big, loud voice came booming out at us. Quickly, everything became perfectly still and silent. There came Vince walking up and down, checking out the players. It was amazing how everyone froze. Nobody moved or said a word. The whole team stood like soldiers waiting for the general to finish inspection and give them orders. As he passed me his whole demeanor changed. A big, broad grin spread across his face. He said, "How are you doing, little lady?" Then, abruptly, Dr. Jekyll came back out, the earth shook, and the general rolled his tank into place. Vince Lombardi certainly was a football general.

I have met interesting people, traveled around the world, attended great parties, met celebrities. We have been invited to attend functions we would not have been included in had it not been for football. We have played in stadiums around the world. There were the great bowl stadiums, and then there was Palermo, Sicily. I'll never forget it. It was hard to imagine that this dirt and rock ground surrounded with bombed-out buildings from World War II was a football field. When the players were tackled they had to pick rocks out of their legs. But did they ever love the game!

We have been associated with three pro teams, eight college teams, and three European teams. We have participated in most major bowls, a Super Bowl, and a Pro Bowl. I have bowl watches for our five sons and their sons, future generation *draft choices*.

Some weekends we would have five games to attend. Four of our boys would be playing, each in a different game, and my husband would be coaching. Our house was either up--we won, or down--we lost. More than likely some had won and some had lost, and the house was in total chaos. Then we would spend hours rehashing the games.

At Christmas we often had three TV sets going at one time because we didn't want to miss one single play of any bowl game. If we had company the men spent their time game-watching and talking about it while the women spent their time in the kitchen.

If some of this sounds a little dated or chauvinistic, IT WAS! During the 50's, 60's, and 70's that's the way it was. I was a young bride by today's experiences and became a coach's wife in the very chauvinistic culture of men's football. This role was the norm then. In truth, women didn't need to know about football. We just kept the food coming, the cars rolling onward to practice, and the schedules in hand as best we could. When football season finally came to an end each year, the big question was, *Where will we be next year?* If we'd had a winning season, we'd get a better offer or stay where we were. If it had been a bad season, we PRAYED we'd get another job.

Our fourth son Tommy was born at the beginning of one such season. I can remember being on the delivery table and the doctor asking me if we'd put our house up for sale yet. WE WERE NOT HAVING A GOOD YEAR! And football season had not even started!

The timing wasn't so great when our other children were born, either. Our oldest son Jon was born the day of the first game of my husband's first high school head coaching job. It was also the first game ever in the history of that school! The school bus carrying my husband and the team came to the hospital on the way to the game. Wally got off the bus and ran in to check to see if the baby had been born. The team sat on the bus chanting, "Hurry, Hurry!" Luckily I had delivered. They went on to the game. Funny, I don't remember if we won or lost that one.

I was due to give birth to our third son. You guessed it. The phone rang, a new job! Wally waited for Danny to arrive, about a week, then off he went! We four followed six weeks later. I just love football! Don't you?

Our second son Steve was born while Wally was a quarterback playing in the pro leagues. Wally came home at 1:00 A.M. after a road game and was upset to find I wasn't there. He thought I was still out playing bridge, and he gave the baby sitter grief until she managed to get it out that I was at the hospital!

Don Shula actually decided our youngest son's birthday. Mini-camp was starting when the baby was due. I thought it would be nice if Wally were present for the birth of at least one son. Shula said, "Go home on March 26th and 27th because we've got all the players coming in on the 28th." So Andrew's birth was induced on the 26th. The next day back went Wally to mini-camp in Miami.

Of all the people I have met one experience stands out. I had a rocky start with one of the most interesting, kind ladies I ever met in the football world. When we joined the Miami Dolphins our fifth son was only a few weeks old. I took the baby to visit my husband so we could look for a house. We stayed in what was then called the *Dolphin Hilton*. Actually, it was a run-down dorm at the practice site.

One day there was a knock at the door, and there stood a dark-haired, rather heavy-set woman wearing a mumu. Thinking she was there to clean up our room, I said, "Just a minute, the baby and I will get out of your way, and you can go ahead and clean." The lady looked at me rather strangely, and then she said, "I am Dorothy Shula, Coach Don Shula's wife." We did eventually become friends.

I have had so many wonderful experiences and learned so much. Most of all, I know that football truly is fun, and the game can be enjoyable.

Why believe the old adage, *We interrupt this marriage, or this relationship, for football season?* What about the motto, **If you can't beat them, join them**! I love it when I enter a room full of men, talk football with them on their level, and watch their reaction.

"How do you know all of this?" they ask.

I just grin.

The purpose of this book is to help women have fun, get involved, and learn the fine points of a great game. Today's women are not going to be bench warmers or stay in the kitchen. We want to interact, to be in the know, to be part of the fun. We want to be in the huddle.

Football is a war game, and there is so much more to watch than just the score or the quarterback. There is strategy involved like in a good chess match. When you see the whole picture, look at the field, and figure out how plays work, the game becomes an exciting match of skill and strategic maneuvers.

I hope this book will help you have as much fun as I have had in all these years of football.

Peggy

7

CHAPTER 1

WHAT WILL I WEAR?

One of the first major college football games I attended was Rice vs. LSU at Rice Stadium in Houston, Texas. My first question was, "What am I going to wear?" I spent the entire game people-watching, trying to see what all the other women were wearing.

I had never seen such an array of clothing, from fantastic designer suits to blue jeans and sweat shirts! Fans had their faces painted, one side purple and one side yellow. Guys were bare-chested. I saw women in designer dress fit for an inauguration and people wearing clothes which barely covered their bodies. That was my first experience of what to wear to a football game. I discovered anything goes!

So, what's the first question you ask when someone says, "Let's go to the game this weekend?" Usually it's, "WHAT WILL I WEAR?"

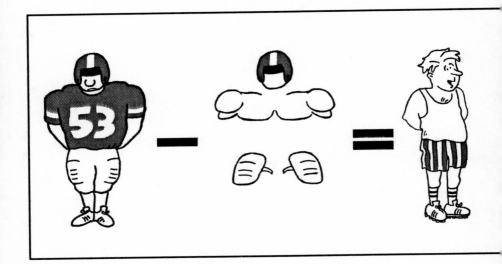

What you see is not always what you get.

Smart women plan their wardrobe, have their colors done, and know their style. When a woman is ready to go somewhere she has an idea of what looks good on her. Style is the result of this basic knowledge and information. This is her foundation.

It is the same in football. We are going to start in the *lingerie department* to give you the basic information. The football player's foundation is a jock strap.

The object of a football game is for one team of eleven players to score more points than the opposing team of eleven players.

"Okay, I'm here. Now where's this 'Pigskin' cutie pie
I keep hearing so much about?"

12

The game is played with an egg-shaped ball eleven inches long which is sometimes called a *pigskin*. It is not made from the skin of a pig anymore, but originally, footballs were.

The pigskin is easily kicked or thrown, but, like a pig, it's sometimes hard to hold and control. This results in fumbles, pass interceptions, blocked punts. The football can be carried, thrown, or kicked. The idea is to get it across the other team's goal line.

"What do you mean you don't have a measuring tape?"

The football field is 100 yards long and 55 yards wide. It is divided into ten, ten yard sections. The middle of the field is the fifty-yard line, graduated to *zero* at the goal line on each end. The field between the goal line and the end line is the end zone. At each end zone are uprights, also called goal posts. The posts are eighteen feet, six inches apart, and the cross bar is ten feet high. These posts are planted at the rear line of the end zone. When the ball is kicked to score points it must go between the goal posts and over the cross bar. When the player crosses over the goal line he is in the end zone which is ten yards deep. Each team has its own end zone. The opposing team scores when it crosses the other team's goal line.

Prior to the actual game the players of both teams move onto the field to warm-up. This is followed by a meeting at the 50-yard line, the middle of the field, of some of the participants you have already seen during warm-up. These are the team captains and the Referee. They shake hands and the Referee takes a coin from his pocket and asks the captain from the visiting team to call the *toss*. He calls *heads* or *tails*. Whoever wins the toss of the coin is given the choice of whether he wants his team to kickoff or receive the ball. The captain of the other team then is given the choice of which end zone he wants his team to defend.

The two teams line up on opposite sides of the 50-yard line in formation for the kickoff. One of the players goes to great lengths to position the football on a little holder and often walks around it to look things over. If he doesn't like what he sees then he will move the ball or start the process over. On windy days the ball often falls off and the player will have to repeat his actions. Once he is satisfied he backs away from the ball and raises his arm in the air to let the Referee know he's ready. On the opposite end of the field the receiver raises his arm to signify that he's ready. The Referee blows his whistle to start the game. As the player begins to run toward the ball he drops his arm, and the players on his team begin to run behind him. This is the *kickoff*. Let the game begin!

The team with the ball is the OFFENSE, and it must move the ball forward 10 yards in four tries to make a first down in order to keep possession of the ball.

Each try is called a DOWN.

If the team advances the ball 10 yards it gets a first down and four more tries, or four more downs, to make another first down. If the team makes less than 10 yards it now has three downs left. This continues until the team scores or fails to make the 10 yards in four tries. Then the team must punt and the other team takes over.

Play focuses around an imaginary line on the field called the *line of scrimmage*. This line separates the OFFENSE and the DEFENSE. The distance between the teams is 11 inches, the length of the football, and is called the *neutral zone*. Each team, OFFENSE and DEFENSE, must have seven players on the line of scrimmage.

Touchdown!

When I was a cheerleader I didn't know anything about football. If someone yelled *Touchdown!* I reached down and touched the ground. Whoever was the cutest player is who I watched. I did know that whoever scored the most points won the game, and if we won there was a party after the game. But I couldn't tell you how points were scored.

So, how do you know who wins the game? There are several ways to score points in football.

TOUCHDOWN
1. When Team A moves the football over Team B's goal line Team A scores a touchdown. (TD). -- 6 points
2. When Team A throws the football over Team B's goal line to a receiver who catches it Team A scores a touchdown. -- 6 points
3. When Team A fumbles in its own end zone and Team B recovers it the TD goes to Team B. -- 6 points
4. If a blocked punt is recovered in the end zone by the opposing team then that team scores a TD.-- 6 points

"Okay...nobody breath!"

SAFETY
5. Tackling the ball carrier while he has the ball in his own end zone is a SAFETY and scores 2 points.

EXTRA POINT/CONVERSION/PAT
6. PAT, Point after touchdown. The kicker must kick the ball through the uprights and over the crossbar to score 1 point. The ball must carried into or thrown and caught in the end zone to score 2 points.

FIELD GOAL
7. Kicking the ball through the uprights over the crossbar from any position on the field scores 3 points.

The extra point or field goal many times decides the winner of a close game. I have seen many games go down to the wire, then someone kicks a field goal in the last seconds of the game to win or misses an extra point to lose.

"All he did was drop the ball."

One of the most exciting games I ever saw was the 1981 Miami Dolphins vs. San Diego Chargers, a play-off game to determine which team went to the Super Bowl. The game was in *sudden death*. The Miami player attempted to score. He fumbled the ball on the four yard line. San Diego picked it up, ran it back to within field goal range, kicked the field goal, and won the game. Miami lost a $50,000.00 bonus and a trip to the Super Bowl, all because a guy was able to plant his foot into a piece of pigskin and put it between two metal posts!

WHO'S GOING TO BE THERE?

When you go to a game you always know which two teams will be playing on game day. However, it's not always as certain when you're faced with the offer of two coaching jobs for two different teams. I remember one move when we didn't know what team we'd be with, and we were already in the middle of packing. The vans were already there!

The movers were carrying the furniture out of the house. Two sons had loaded a truck and were headed toward Utah. We thought we were going to Brigham Young University. Another son was headed to Germany with a return ticket to Utah. My youngest son and I were to follow the moving van.

The phone rang. I had to find the phone which was somewhere under the stuff to be moved. It was Bum Phillips, the head coach of the Houston Oilers. I located my husband who was on the back of the moving van and called him to the phone. I tried to make sense of the conversation which went like this, "Certainly, I'd love to coach for the Houston Oilers. But I've just taken a position with BYU and the movers are here. We're almost loaded...well, you're right, the movers could come to Houston instead of Utah."

My husband hung up and told me that he was flying to Houston for an interview before proceeding to Utah.

"Do you think you'd like to live in Houston?" he asked.

Then he asked the movers if it would be okay for us to start out headed for Utah and then decide to change our destination.

"Could we let you know which way to go when we arrive in Lincoln, Nebraska--Texas or Utah?" he asked. I left, not knowing where we would end up. We did end up in Utah.

When Wally came back from Houston he told me the story about his interview. The first thing Bum said to him was, "Boy, if you're going to work here you've gotta take off that suit and tie." Wally always second-guessed himself about his decision to choose Utah. He thought Bum Phillips was quite a man.

SO, WHO IS THERE, WHEN YOU ARRIVE AT THE GAME?

The *tailgaters* are found in the parking lots of most college and pro games. The Notre Dame parking lot is full all season. I don't think those people ever go home. The tailgaters are serious fans, serious about food and drink. Some of these folks park their RV's in the lots the night before the game. They want to be ready, and what better way is there to be ready than a party before and after the game? The idea of tailgating is to get to the game early, see your friends, talk about your team, drink beer, and enjoy yourself. This is a *tradition*. Of course, some of these fans never make it into the game. Those fans who do show up are a colorful group.

The Fans

First, there are those folks who come to see the game in all modes of dress and outfits and attitudes.

There's the woman dressed to the *nines* with perfectly-styled hair and manicured nails who likes the half-time show better than the game.

Then there's the *organizer* who wears the right colors, leads the cheers, and insists that everyone else in her group join her.

Next, there's the guy who bets on the game not caring which team wins or loses as long as he beats the point spread.

Somewhere there's a guy who knows every player, recites all the statistics, knows the Four Horsemen from Notre Dame, and he tells you everything he knows.

Unfortunately, there's always the fan who is totally obnoxious. He has a passion for the players and his team, and he screams, yells, never sits down, spills his drink down your back, and becomes more obnoxious as the game progresses. We may need CPR for him at the end of the game.

Usually there's a party animal. He or she is only there to celebrate, pass around the drinks, see who's there, and be the center of attention. This person doesn't even know who is playing.

Last, but not least, there's the person who absolutely knows nothing but has read the sports page today about each team and quotes it continuously. He probably has cheat sheet notes written on his cuffs. He is trying to impress and hasn't a clue.

NOW FOR THE REAL LINE-UP

The OFFENSIVE TEAM is the team with the ball. Their object is to run with the ball or to pass it to a receiver until they cross the goal line and score a touchdown.

The DEFENSIVE TEAM is the team without the ball. They try to knock, push, shove, or tackle the offensive team to keep them from taking the ball across the line, thus preventing a touchdown.

SPECIAL TEAMS are just that. They're selected to perform a specific task. These are OFFENSIVE teams and DEFENSIVE teams who are not playing regular offense or defense, as in running or passing plays. They are part of the kicking teams who play when some form of kicking the ball is required.

The kickoff team kicks the ball at the beginning of the game and at the beginning of the 2nd half. The kickoff return team receives the ball at the kickoff and attempts to return it for a TD. The special teams perform these same roles after each TD and/or extra point.

The punting team punts the ball when their offense has failed to make a first down in four attempts. The punt return team receives the ball and attempts to return it.

The place kick team is on the field only for the for the extra point attempt after a TD or the field goal attempt.

"I can't wear these...they don't match."

HOW DO YOU RECOGNIZE THE TWO TEAMS?

All teams have *home* and *travel* jerseys. The home jersey color is usually the dominate team color. Enter now tradition and superstition. The team, the owners, the coaches, and not least of all, the fans know for certain that wearing this jersey brings the team luck. Sometimes both teams have the same colors. In this case, the home team has the privilege of choosing their preferred jerseys which, in most instances, is the home jersey in their dominant team color.

THE OFFENSE POSITIONS

The *quarterback* is the leader of the team and calls the plays. The *center* snaps the ball to the *quarterback*. *Guards* line up on either side of the *center--left guard* on his left, *right guard* on his right. The *tackles* line up on either side of the guard--*left tackle* on the left and *right tackle* on the right. *Tight ends* line up to the outside of the *tackles*. *Wide receivers* spread out 10-15 yards to the sides of the offensive line. *Running backs* line up behind the *quarterback*. This is called the *back field*.

THE DEFENSE POSITIONS

The *defensive tackles* line up opposite the *offense* on the defensive line. *Defensive ends* line up opposite the *offense* on the defensive line. *Linebackers* line up two to three yards in back of their own *tackles* and *ends*. *Cornerbacks* line up opposite the opposing team's *wide receivers*. *Safeties* are the safety net in case of a pass. They line up 8-10 yards behind the line of scrimmage.

OFFENSE

WIDE RECEIVER

TIGHT END

TACKLE

GUARD

RUNNING BACK

QUARTERBACK

CEN

RUNNING BACK

GUARD

TACKLE

WIDE RECEIVER

MCCARTH

DEFENSE

DEFENSIVE END

DEFENSIVE TACKLE

DEFENSIVE TACKLE

DEFENSIVE END

LINEBACKER

LINEBACKER

LINEBACKER

CORNERBACK

SAFETY

SAFETY

CORNERBACK

" They all seem like tight ends to me."

HOW DO YOU RECOGNIZE THE PLAYERS?

It's all in the numbers! Usually, the *quarterbacks* and *kickers* wear jerseys with numbers from 1-19. *Running backs* and *defensive backs* wear numbers from 20-49. *Centers* and *linebackers* wear numbers 50-59. *Offensive guards*, *tackles* and *defensive linemen* wear numbers 60-79. In general, the bigger the player, the bigger the number!

Defensive linemen, *offensive guards* and *offensive tackles* line up across from each other. They heckle each other with name calling, challenges, anything they can do to distract the other team. If this works it breaks the opponent's concentration causing him to miss crucial moves or make mistakes in clutch situations. *Wide receivers* and *tight ends* wear numbers 80-89. The job of the *wide receiver* is to catch the passes thrown by the *quarterback*. The *tight end* either catches the ball or blocks for the runners. He is the end man on the line.

"Calm down guys, can't we just talk about it?"

WHO ARE THOSE OTHER PEOPLE ON THE FIELD?

The CHAIN GANG is in charge of moving the chain up and down the field to indicate the position of the football on the field. The long pole which displays numbers from one to four signifies the down coming up. You can recognize the gang by their bright colored vests.

Last, but not least, THE OFFICIALS! They are called *The Zebras* by the players. These are the guys in the black and white-stripped shirts with whistles around their necks and the dreaded yellow flags in their pockets. They have to be in top-shape to run up and down the field constantly. They keep the game running smoothly.

There are seven different officials in professional games, usually six in college games, and four in high school games. They are the most disliked people on the field because everybody in the stands know more than they do. Off the field they are nice guys.

"He must not realize that there is a higher authority."

THE COACH

The coach and the coaching staff design the plays. They spend many bleary hours watching tapes of the other teams to design strategies in an effort to beat the opponent in every area--offense, defense, and the kicking game.

Football is truly a war game. Coaches win anyway they can, sorting through their opponent's trash baskets, stealing play books, or spying on practices from a cherry picker. Of course, all this is illegal! If they get caught they're in big trouble. There are too many stories about the lengths some coaches will go to win the game to include in this book. Not many battles have been better fought than those on a football field. General George Patton would have been a great coach and Knute Rockne, the legendary Notre Dame coach, a great general.

WHEN DOES IT START?

Coaches' wives react to GAME TIME in every different way imaginable. The game's playing time is actually sixty minutes, but that sixty minutes can last three hours. Personally I would stall to get to the game late, often arriving when it was almost over. This way I avoided an attack of nerves.

A well-known coach's wife who always arrives on time for games tells a story about one trip she remembers. She was running late. She hopped in her car wearing a mink coat, her hair in curlers, and raced off to the game. She had car trouble on the way, and she had to get out on the road and hitchhike, still in curlers and the mink. Some nice folks who picked her up on their way to the game were amazed to discover when they arrived at the stadium that she was the head coach's wife.

Then, there are the eager-beaver types of coach's wives who arrive early and literally pace the sidelines and watch the warmups acting like one of the coaches.

There are two kinds of football time--the length of the season and the length of the game. The season for the National Football League starts in July and ends in February. Typically, college seasons start in August and end in early January.

Let's talk about what goes on during that sixty minutes of playing time besides beer runs, bathroom breaks, and cheerleader-gawking.

A football game is basically played in sixty minutes. The sixty minutes are broken down into four fifteen-minute quarters. High school quarters are only 12 minutes long. There is a *half-time* between the second and third quarters. Some people only come to watch what happens at *half-time* because of the show and/or marching bands.

There are two clocks which run during the game. One is on the scoreboard, and the officials have the other which is really the OFFICIAL CLOCK!

The game starts when the Referee signals the start of play. The clock may start and stop with each play or may run continuously on some plays. The Officials use a whistle to stop play at which time the clock stops. The clock can be an advantage or a disadvantage. If your team is winning it is an advantage, if you're losing it's a disadvantage.

"Where did these guys learn to tell time?"

The clock is stopped for many reasons. Some of these are:

- Incomplete pass
- Infraction of a rule
- After a score
- After a kickoff
- At the end of each quarter
- For TV commercials
- At the whim of the officials
- After an injury
- Time outs
- Overtime
- Sudden death

This is why sixty minutes may last THREE hours.

TIME TO PLAY!

The OFFENSIVE TEAM goes into a *huddle* which looks a lot like a group hug, and the quarterback tells them what play he is going to call next.

I attended one of the first football games played in Japan. When the team went into the huddle all the fans stood up and leaned forward and everything got very quiet. They were TRYING to listen to what was happening in the huddle.

Talk about *timing* and *timeouts*. We have had some bad timing during my husband's career. We were at the University of Kentucky. The carpet had just been laid in our new home. This was just before Thanksgiving. We were looking forward to really enjoying the holidays and relaxing after the months of building. Wally came home about 3 o'clock that afternoon. I thought he had come to see the carpet. He sat down, wrote something on a piece of paper, and handed it to me. The head coach had been fired which meant we had all been fired! So much for the new home and relaxing holidays! Wally told me later that he didn't have the nerve to tell me, hence the note. Martha Bradshaw, the head coach's wife, came over the next day and wisely counseled me to "Never get attached to a house in this business."

It took a long time before we decided to build another house. This home was our dream home. I had saved the plans for years. The house was about 95% completed. Wally got a call from the Detroit Lions offering him a job. We certainly could not pass up a chance to coach in the pro's! The clock had run out. We never moved into that house. We moved to Detroit.

"Not that bomb!"

54

SO WHAT GOES ON DURING THIS GAME TIME?

The coaches, the generals, call this frenzy *strategy*. The minute one game is over the coaches start planning for the next game. How can they beat the next team? What *secret play* can they come up with? In actuality there is no secret play--it's in the execution of the play.

Charlie McClendon, a great coach at LSU for many years, once said: "If they can't score, they can't win." That's defensive strategy.

My husband, on the other hand, believes in the passing game. He likes to throw the ball. Long, high passes down the field are referred to as *bombs*. He used this offensive strategy so often one year that his team actually gave him a real bomb trophy following the game. The inscription on the trophy read *Air English*. The University of Pittsburg defeated South Carolina 38-6 in that game at the Gator Bowl in Jacksonville, Florida. Dan Marino completed four bombs for four touchdowns in that game.

The two teams try to trick each other by the way they line up and the plays they call. In today's world the offensive and defensive plays are fed into computers for statistical, strategic evaluation. Players are watched for their tendencies--which foot does he step with first, does the quarterback cock his head before he throws, or does he move his wrist if he's going to run?

FOOTBALL HAS BECOME A SCIENCE!

Anything can be used to fake-out the other team--a crib sheet on the quarterback's arm, a head set in his helmet, a coach on the sidelines sending monkey signals to the players. Whatever it takes to gain an advantage is used.

Who do you watch to figure out the game plan and predict what play will be called? The best way is to watch the offensive line.

First, find the ball on the field. This is the line of scrimmage.

Now look for the CENTER. He's right over the ball, remember him, the big guy with his rear end in the air. He's right in the center of the offensive line.

When he snaps the ball to the quarterback the offensive line will either jump forward to try to knock down the defensive guys facing them or step back and act like brick walls to try to stop the defensive players from rushing the passer.

If they jump forward it's usually a run. If they step backward it's probably going to be a pass. This is where the trick comes in. Sometimes they step back only to surge forward to try to fool the defensive team.

In the meantime the defensive team is trying to figure out what the offense is going to do by the way they've lined up. If they think the quarterback is going to throw the ball they might *blitz* which means lots of the defensive players try to tackle the quarterback at once. If it looks like they're going to run with the ball the defense tries to gang up on the runner.

"Just throw the $* \# @ \sim$ ball and get it over with!"

WHO HAS THE BALL?

Have you ever looked at the field and wondered? If the offense isn't passing they're running. So to fool the defense the quarterback pretends to hand the ball to a running back in such a way that you can't tell who has the ball, then he keeps the ball and runs with it.

There may be several running plays where the quarterback hands the ball to another back. When the quarterback actually keeps the ball himself, that's the *Quarterback Sneak* or the *Quarterback Option.*

The quarterback keeps the ball many times to throw it, not just to run with it. He backs up into what is called a *pocket.* When he does this the offensive linemen form a semicircle to protect him and give him time to throw the ball. There are two choices. Pass or run!

Can you figure out which will happen? It really isn't too complicated. Pass or run. So, why does it take three hours to play the game and a whole week to plan the game?

Remember, he who scores the most points, wins!

CHAPTER 4

WHO'S THE BOSS HERE?

Rules are meant to be broken. Women often take this literally. We sometimes see things differently from men. Women know the rules but go on and do what they want to do anyway. It's okay to talk about your best friend, but no one else better talk about her! Logic does not apply when a woman confronts the Officials. The head coach can scream, yell, threaten, and so can the players. One hundred thousand fans can boo from the stands, and the TV commentator can be incredulous, but the Referee is the boss and nothing changes his mind. Once the call is made it's written in stone.

Once you know how the game works and who's in charge then you can understand the seriousness of the calls. I remember B.J. Arnsparger who is the wife of Bill Arnsparger, recently defense coordinator of the Miami Dolphins. B.J is normally a lady-like, mild-mannered person. But come football season during a game her language and her screaming at the Ref is not repeatable. I always thought B.J. would make a good coach.

"I could use some of these at home"

The officials are the ones who keep the game running smoothly by providing law and order. They do that by making sure the players don't break the rules. When players do break the rules it's called an INFRACTION, and a penalty results. The rule book gives 67 infractions with a penalty for each. Ladies, can you imagine working for a control freak with 67 rules which change in some way every year?

How do you know an infraction has been called? You'll hear the crowd shouting, booing, or cheering, depending on which team they're supporting. And then you'll hear the announcer say, *Flag on the play*. Your first clue is a bright yellow handkerchief the Official has thrown onto the playing field to signal the call. This handkerchief is not a part of his outfit. No silk tie or kerchief, this is his banner of glory thrown onto the field to show who's in control of the battle. In case you miss the flag you can't miss the whistle. Officials dearly love to blow their whistles!

I've included those infractions which are most frequently broken. Knowing them will keep you aware of what's happening on the playing field.

UNSPORTSMANLIKE CONDUCT/PERSONAL FOUL
This is a judgment call. It's used if a player curses, kicks another player in the groin, or piles on, in other words, doesn't behave like a gentleman. The penalty is 15 yards.

OFFSIDE

This is a common call. Movement by any player, offense or defense, across the line of scrimmage before the ball is snapped is an offside infraction call. The penalty is five yards.

ENCROACHMENT

Encroachment is called when the defense causes the offense to move offside before the ball is snapped. The penalty is five yards.

CLIPPING

No one likes to be hit from behind. In football, one player cannot go after another player from behind hitting him on the knees or legs. This is unsportsmanlike conduct specifically called *clipping*. The defense <u>can</u> tackle a running player from behind. The penalty is fifteen yards.

OFFENSIVE HOLDING/ DEFENSIVE HOLDING

This is illegal use of the hands. There is a complicated list of ways in which players may not block, grab, or contact another player. A player can't use his hands to *hug* another player, to slap him, pop his jock strap. This is also a judgment call which is used frequently giving the fans a chance to yell and scream about the Ref's calls. The penalty is fifteen yards when called on the defense and ten yards when called on the offense.

FACE MASK

The face mask covers the face and is attached to the helmet. Thou shalt not grab or hold the face mask, twist it, or turn it because the player's head is inside! If a player grabs the face mask unintentionally that's a five yard penalty. If he grabs and twists it or throws a player on the ground by holding onto it intentionally, that's a fifteen yard penalty.

ROUGHING THE KICKER/ROUGHING THE PASSER

Thou shalt not touch the kicker after he's kicked the ball, or the passer after he's thrown the pass. The penalty is fifteen yards.

DELAY OF THE GAME

The offense has to snap the ball within twenty-five seconds after the Ref signals the clock to start indicating the game is in play. Sometimes the offensive team deliberately waits too long in order to buy them extra time. They may want to change their *strategy*. The penalty is five yards.

INTENTIONAL GROUNDING

It is against the rules for the passer to throw the ball away in order to avoid a loss of yardage. Sometimes he can get away with this when there is a receiver in the vicinity of his throw. The penalty is ten yards and loss of the down.

CHAPTER 5

WHERE WILL WE GO AFTER THE GAME?

TO THE VICTORS GO THE SPOILS!!!!!!!

Money **Rings** **Trophies** **Watches** **Trips** **Parties**

The season ends with playoffs and championship games at all levels after the regular season. There are the sought-after Bowl Games. No matter which one you attend they are all filled with excitement, parties, and fun. We'll start with the Professional teams.

The culmination of the professional football season is the Super Bowl which, for professional teams, players, coaches, could be related in women's terms to an unlimited shopping spree on Rodeo Drive. It is spectacular!

Pre-season play begins in August. These are just practice games. Regular season play begins in September and runs through December. The 32 National Football League teams play the other teams in their respective leagues, The American Football Conference and The National Football Conference. Each team plays a 16-game schedule. Six teams from each conference earn *playoff* spots. Finally, after these we are down to two playoff games. One team from each conference emerges the winner and gets to play in the Super Bowl.

Now the fun begins. The Super Bowl is scheduled for the last Sunday in January. The winning team receives the Vince Lombardi Trophy. Each member of the team receives an expensive diamond-studded Super Bowl ring and a $75,000 + personal bonus.

The Super Bowl is viewed on TV in 175 countries and by over 130 million people in the United States. Fifty million of these viewers are women, thus Real Women want to know football!

Super Bowl parties across America rank right next to Christmas and Thanksgiving as far as the amount of food and cheer which is served.

Super Bowl week is one filled with events. My list contains only a small number of the dozens and dozens of these events.

Each NFL team hosts a Hospitality Room in their hotels. Celebrities are in and out of these rooms all week long.

The media networks host Hospitality Rooms and parties. These events are usually by invitation only.

Sporting Goods companies and large corporations hold parties and use this week to entertain clients. You would be hard-pressed not to find a party somewhere, even out on the streets by the hotels!

On the Friday night before Super Bowl Sunday the Commissioner of the National Football League hosts the *Grand-daddy* of all parties. This epicurean extravaganza is rivaled by no other party. All of the *Who's Who* in the sports world attend. The clothes are stunning and the food is outstanding. Several thousand people attend. Media coverage is everywhere. Hollywood, eat your heart out! This soiree rivals the best on Oscar Night!

Finally, on Sunday game day arrives. After the game the parties continue, especially in the winning team's city.

THE PRO BOWL

The End! This event ends the professional season. The Pro Bowl is played in Aloha Stadium in Honolulu, Hawaii, one week after the Super Bowl. Party on!

The men who coach the Pro Bowl teams are the runner-up coaches from the NFC and the AFC Championship games. The team members for the Pro Bowl teams are the best players from each NFC and AFC team. They are selected by their peers. Thus, a team comprised of American Conference members plays a team comprised of National Conference members, AFC vs. NFC.

Each team stays at a luxury hotel on the ocean with a magnificent setting. There is always a party somewhere all week long. Of course, there has to be a little practice time thrown in for good measure. The winner of the game gets a substantial bonus. The loser also gets a bonus. Getting to go to Hawaii in February with all-expenses-paid should be enough.

This game officially closes the NFL season. Football widows, *coaches' wives*, can enjoy March, April, May, and June. Training camp starts again in July.

Don't forget the pro football draft is held in April. This draft is where the college seniors are chosen by the pro teams. The money these players get for signing is incredible. It would last a lifetime. **Pro Football is Big Business.**

COLLEGE BOWL GAMES

Many loyal college fans look forward to the smell of orange blossoms, rose petals, or Cajun cooking at the end of the college regular season. These fans try to tie Christmas vacation to a trip to watch their team play in Miami, New Orleans, Pasadena, Dallas, San Antonio, Phoenix, Hawaii. There are twenty-five different cities that host college football bowl games. These 25 games are played during the last two weeks of December and on January 1 and 2. All games are televised which gives you something to do during the Christmas holidays.

By winning most or all of the regular season games a good college team can look forward to spending Christmas and New Year's, all expenses paid, at some prestigious bowl game. The College Football National Championship has been decided until recently in a January 1st or 2nd Bowl game. The bowl system is undergoing changes in order to schedule the last game of the season on January 4 in the Fiesta Bowl which happens to be my favorite bowl. Hopefully, this contest will match the #1 and #2 ranked college teams to decide the National Championship.

A normal bowl week for the typical fan consists of hosted breakfasts, lunches, dinners, and dances, especially on New Year's Eve. University-sponsored events, Alumni events, bowl-sponsored events, pictures with the teams and coaches are the highlights of the activities during the week of the game. Media coverage is not quite like Super Bowl coverage, but the press is still there. When the rival teams are from two different states the Governors wager publicly. Over-zealous fans try to out-boast and out-party each other. If you attend all the events you can be certain to gain five pounds.

Bowls like to host big schools because they always have thousands of fans in attendance, and since Notre Dame has one of the largest Bowl followings in college football they are usually always invited to a Bowl game. At this level the game focuses on University and State honor and prestige, not money. The University does receive money from the bowl game, however. The teams playing in these bowl games view these games very seriously and work very hard. The fans enjoy the week as do the coaches' wives. The coaches and the players are too busy trying to win. When we played in the Japan Bowl my husband spent most of his time getting ready for the game. He didn't even see Japan. The game could have been at home for all he knew. The players and coaches do attend some of the functions, but winning is really all that is on their minds.

HIGH SCHOOL CHAMPIONSHIPS

Every state has a high school play-off system leading to a state championship. These are very serious undertakings for many young men. Three of our sons, Jon and Steve at Brother Rice High

School in Birmingham, Michigan, and Andrew at St. Louis High School in Honolulu, Hawaii, have been on teams which won their state championships. This was the highlight of their high school careers. Our five sons, Jon, Steve, Dan, Thomas and Andrew have been awarded four-year football scholarships to college. Mothers, get those kids to practice and save yourself some tuition!

Many valuable lessons are learned on the high school football field. Many valuable friendships are made, and many wonderful memories that last a lifetime stem from high school. Attitude, leadership, persistence, and teamwork are instilled in high school. Not all young men will make it to the college or pro level in football, so being on a high school team can be a very rewarding experience. There may not be as many parties surrounding the high school championship, but you can bet it is as important to these young men as the Super Bowl is to the Green Bay Packers.

Remember, Real Moms know football, too, and encourage their sons to get out on that field. We have a saying in our house when we're asked if the boys HAVE to play football, "No, certainly not, they can move!"

THE REAL STORY

A common thread runs through all the experiences I have had relating to football. It's called a love of adventure! We have had fun, moved to new places, met new people. I've been through highs and lows, the winning and the losing. I've watched people on top fall to the bottom and seen people come from the pits to the heights. Knowing the real truth about situations and being able to keep my mouth shut has been a real part of it. These stories are about real people I have been lucky to know. I've seen from the inside what really goes on in the world of football.

Several places I've lived stand out in my mind, Brigham Young University, Virginia Tech, and, of course, England, and Germany. But Italy was the most enjoyable one and the one where we had the most fun. After our twenty-hour flight to Italy we were picked up and taken directly to the football field for practice. They wanted Wally to start coaching immediately. What we saw looked like a dirt field with rocks and stones all over it. The area was still in ruins from World War II. It looked like a ghetto park. This was the playing field. The Italians were very excited about the sport. They loved it. Our son Danny was the quarterback. He threw the ball fifty-two times in one game. The first time he threw a touchdown pass they were so excited, screaming and yelling with Italian exuberance. Every time after that when he threw the ball they would chant: "Dan-ny, Dan-ny, Dan-ny..." The more he threw the ball, the more they chanted and yelled.

Our first road game was in Agrigenta. We were all on two busses. Behind us followed a long line of cars, the fans and the players' families. We were instructed to stop half-way for a small, pre-game meal. We arrived at a picnic area, and all the Italian mothers piled out of the cars with awesome baskets of food. Wally kept yelling, "We can't eat all that, no, no, no... we can't eat all that!" About an hour and a half later after having consumed carloads of wonderful Italian food we were now late for the game. We arrived about half-an-hour late, and the other team had waited for us. It turned out to be a great game, and we won. However, the coach wasn't very pleased about the pre-game feast.

This team went twelve and zero, and it was the first time they had won the National Football League in Italy. It was the most exciting, most fun group of players--lots of camaraderie and no prima donnas. When it came to football they just loved it.

During our time in Palermo there was a water shortage. We had ten minutes in the morning and ten minutes in the afternoon to do laundry and take showers. One day after practice during this shortage the players were talking about going to get in the spa.

I thought, Oh, to get in a hot tub. Where can this possibly be?

"Sure, you can go, come follow us," they said.

We started a caravan up the side of a mountain, and I thought, This must be some elegant, beautiful spa I haven't heard about! We went down a little dirt road and I began to think they were pulling my leg, that it was a joke. We got out of the cars and followed a little path through trees to a VOLCANIC HOT TUB! The players went there three times a week. The heat from the volcano warmed this huge pool of mineral water. When you got out your muscles were relaxed and your skin felt like velvet. It was a wonderful, natural spa.

When we first got to Italy we didn't speak Italian so we had an interpreter. Wally, being the *General* type, would yell and scream, including a few curse words that they understood perfectly. But they didn't understand his English. So he named all the players with nicknames which they then began to call each other. One guy was *Smoker* because he smoked all the time. There was a *Big Joe* and a *Little Joe*. The players didn't resent the nicknames. They liked them and started to use them themselves.

I'll never forget the Italians' joy for life, food, volcanic hot tubs, and, most of all, no matter where they had to play it, football!

The opportunity to meet so many interesting people had to be the highlight of all those years. Everybody hears stories about coaches throughout the football community, good stories, crazy stories, and negative ones. Probably the biggest mistake in first impressions I made was about Jimmy Johnson. When Jimmy left the University of Pittsburgh Wally became the coach. I didn't know Jimmy yet but had heard a lot of stories about what a great coach he was. Then I met him in New Orleans one evening on Bourbon Street. He was dressed in a wild, flowered shirt, his hair tousled, and I thought, Well, I'm not so impressed. So this is the Jimmy Johnson everybody's talking about? He doesn't look like he's so great.

I certainly was wrong. He went on to become the head coach of the University of Miami Hurricanes, the Dallas Cowboys, and the Miami Dolphins. In the process he won a national championship and two Super Bowls. Now you don't see him with a hair out of place.

Jerry Glanville used to be with the Atlanta Falcons and the Detroit Lions. He's a very wild and crazy guy who dresses in all black. Jerry left tickets for Elvis Presley at all the box offices for the day Elvis decided to attend one of his games. Even before the days when he wore black, he rode a motorcycle which was rather uncommon at the time. When we were with the Detroit Lions he used to come to our house, put our kids on his motorcycle, and drive them around our large, circular drive. This would scare me to death.

Al Davis, the owner of the Oakland Raiders, has always been a tough person. Once he kicked Wally out of one of his practices. Wally had gone to visit one of the coaches. Al either didn't know who he was or thought he was spying for one of the other pro teams. A year or so later the Raiders won the Super Bowl, and we happened to be at a party afterward. Al was sitting alone and Wally walked over to talk with him. When I saw this my first thoughts were that this owner who had just won the Super Bowl was going to remember that he'd kicked Wally out of a practice, and it would be an unpleasant conversation given Al's reputation for not getting along with people. I was surprised that the guy who had just won the Super Bowl was sitting alone, in the first place. But he was glad to see Wally, happy that someone had come over to talk to him. Al wasn't at all what I expected him to be. That night he was really a nice guy.

Woody Hayes, former head coach at Ohio State University, had a bad reputation. People said how rough he was, and some of them never forgot the incident or forgave him for hitting a player on the sidelines. Yet people never knew that Woody helped a lot of others, especially kids, and contributed to charities. We do tend to remember just the negative things and forget the good some coaches do. But Woody had his quirks. He didn't like it when other coaches attended his talks at recruiting functions because he thought it interfered with his recruiting efforts. It was his show and he wanted to be the center of attention. So he banned coaches. Once Wally just wanted to hear Woody speak so he went into the room wearing his jacket from Virginia Tech where he was coaching. Woody stopped his speech, looked at him, and said, "Hey, boy, are those your school colors?" Woody made a big deal of the fact that Wally was there invading his space, so to speak.

LaVell Edwards, the head coach at Brigham Young University, had Wally fly to Utah to interview for a coaching position which we accepted. It turned out to be one of the nicest and most enjoyable places we ever lived. When Wally arrived in Provo, Utah, at BYU which is a Mormon university, he had to be interviewed by their *twelve apostles*. He and LaVell went to Salt Lake City into one of the large Mormon buildings to a room with an executive table around which the *twelve* were sitting. Wally expected to be asked about his coaching philosophy, his tactics, his experience. Instead, they asked questions of a personal nature, "Do you drink, smoke, run around with women?" When he said, "No! No! No!" to these questions they said, "Well, okay, you're hired. Have a good time." LaVell's wife, Patty, is one of the best coaches' wives I have ever met. She's generous and giving. She writes a weekly sports column for the paper in Provo. She's always been involved in football, never misses a game, and yet she is still a nervous wreck, chewing her nails and getting upset with the crowd if they are critical of her husband or the team. She travels with LaVell to all the games. They're a great football couple.

Tom Osborne, former head coach at Nebraska, is another very nice person. He's down to earth, real, no phony. His fame hasn't gone to his head. When we were at Nebraska we were the youngest coaches on the staff, the *new kids on the block*.

It's hard to be famous because you can't go out to eat in peace. People want Tom's autograph, and he is interrupted constantly as he tries to eat. One night Tom was leaving a restaurant as Wally and I were going in. I will never forget this. He introduced me to his wife because we had not met and then said, "We'll go in and sit down with you for a few minutes."I know that was very difficult for him because he'd just tried to get away from a dozen people. But he did go back in with us and have dessert. That was very thoughtful. One never hears anything negative about Tom.

One of our first, big time coaching jobs was at the University of Arkansas. Frank Broyles was the head coach. Raymond Berry was on the staff. Jimmy Johnson had just left to take a head coaching job. Two of the other coaches were Billy Kinard who went on to be head coach at Ole Miss and Charlie Coffee who went to Virginia Tech. It was a great place to experience the game and learn from these expert coaches. Frank was an excellent leader, and Arkansas football was at an all-time high. Frank had all the coaches and their wives or girlfriends over to his house after the games, win or lose. Dinner was pot luck. He always invited the press, a smart move on his part. This made him available to them so they printed his view of the game even when we lost. He was a good friend of Darrell Royal, the head coach at The University of Texas. Those two would really go at it.

There are many tough rules in the NFL. It does, however, take tough rules to control head-strong coaches and players. Some head coaches go a little overboard in legislating their charges. At one NFL camp an assistant was unable to leave a practice to attend his daughter's wedding. Another year a coach's wife died. Only the wives attended the funeral. The coaches weren't allowed to go because they were preparing for a game. The things which happened and continue to happen *behind closed doors* during the season would amaze, astonish, and perhaps, anger people, if they knew about them.

There are the coaches with big egos who think they are never wrong. Once an NFL coach took everyone on his staff out to eat when we were in Hawaii at the Pro Bowl. He ordered *vichyssoise* which is a cold potato soup. When it was served he tasted it and said to the waiter, "This soup is cold, take it back, I don't want it." Nobody dared say a word even through they knew the soup was supposed to be cold. Nobody was going to tell him he was wrong!

One practice day my son Tommy, who was in the seventh grade, was out on the field with some of the Dolphin players. Don Shula, the head coach, was walking across the field. Tommy didn't realize he was there, and in missing a throw to a player, hit Shula right in the nose with the ball, knocking him to the ground. Shula immediately got up, composed himself, and went to the dressing room sporting a bad bloody nose. The next day at practice he announced he was cutting the youngest player on the team. Tommy English was no longer allowed to throw footballs on the field. Don is a great coach and loves kids, but he doesn't allow any horsing around on the field.

Head coaches from dozens of colleges had been invited to the Dallas Cowboys' party week. All week long, everytime they saw

Lou Holtz they saw Father Joyce, president of Notre Dame. They saw Lou in a golf cart--they saw Father Joyce with him. They saw Father Joyce at lunch--they saw Lou with him. Everyone was curious. In time the head coach's position became available at Notre Dame. Guess who was hired? Lou Holtz always was a step ahead.

Jackie Sherrill was the head coach at the University of Pittsburgh. He was one of the smoothest talkers and best recruiters around. Once when they were recruiting a certain kid he told Wally, "On recruiting day, I want to be there bright and early, at 7:30 A.M. We can go in the house at 8:00. We can be the first ones there. I want to get this kid." So they drove out to the boy's house at 7:30. Out in front of the house was a brand new car. Jackie and Wally looked at each other. They sat there until 8:00, got out of the car to go in the house to sign the player. At that moment, the door opened and out walked a coach smoking a cigar. He shook the boy's hand and said, "Glad to have you aboard." I think Jackie turned the coach in.

One year we were at the play-offs in Dallas. The Minnesota Vikings were there. Carl Eller, who was a huge player and well-known for his ability, was stopped in the lobby for his autograph.

He told the kids to get away from him as he had to get on the bus. The head coach at the time was Bud Grant. Carl could have knocked him over with one bone-crushing block. But Bud, with a look that meant absolute authority, and that's all it took, one look, signaled to Carl who immediately got the message. He walked back to the kids and said, "Here, let me sign that for you." So not all coaches have to yell to get their point across! Bud Grant could be tough with a look.

Some coaches think they're invisible. I remember one coach's wife whose husband was having an affair. He was the head coach at a large school in a small town. Very visible. Very prominent. One day, she said, "You know, it makes me so mad! He thinks he's invisible and that no one knows him or sees what he does." He would park his car in front of a small motel just outside town. Everyone knew it was his, could see it there, and knew who was there with him. It seemed like he thought no one could see it, but everybody could and so could his wife.

Once when we were in Dallas a very prominent coach at that time told us not to get in line out front at a popular restaurant which was always extremely crowded. He said we should go around to the back door and we'd be seated immediately. One night we did this, and I noticed that this coach's wife was in the line out front. I thought, If she's in line, why aren't we in line? But we went around back, and as we walked in the back door the coach came out with his girl friend while his wife waited in line at the front door.

There was another coach we saw at dinner with a young woman. Later we mentioned to the coach's wife that we'd seen her husband and daughter. We learned afterward that the couple only had sons.

It's amazing how some people in the public eye think others can't see what they are doing, and even more amazing is the thought that perhaps they don't care if others do know.

A lot of people think that pro-coaching is very exciting and that the wives have an equally exciting, fast track, glamorous life. Well, it's not exactly that way. Your husband may be absent six months out of the year. This is not easy, but it's the perks which you might not have otherwise that make it bearable. You get to take trips at the end of the season, go to play-offs and bowl games. If you win, there is a large monetary bonus involved. If it's a Super

Bowl, it could be as much as $75,000 for each of the players and the coaches.

I remember when the owner of the Detroit Lions, William Clay Ford and his wife Elizabeth, who is a lovely woman, took all the coaches' wives out to a wonderful, yearly luncheon. Before we arrived it was announced at the restaurant that we would be there that day for lunch. There was a big sign welcoming us. I overheard someone say, in a disappointed voice, "THOSE are the Detroit Lion's wives? Well, they're not so glamorous!" As it was, we weren't so glamorous, just ordinary people.

The college football coaches' convention takes place every year during the second week of January. Most of the coaches go to this convention. They are like old women sitting around or standing in the lobby, a beehive of noise and confusion. *What job is going to open? Who's going where? Who do you know who can do me a favor? Did you hear what ... did?* It's a four-day gossip and meetings session, worse than any hen-party you can imagine. This is what goes on behind the scenes in football–the back-stabbing, deals making, job jostling among the coaches. Who's leaving, who's going where? The politics put in play at this convention is intense. Coaches call ahead, recommend themselves, recommend each other. It's quite a fraternity, but usually one without any loyalty.

During these years I have met so many players, many unforgettable. Some were role models for our sons. Some had outstanding talent. And some may have been great players, but you wouldn't want to take them home to meet Mom.

When we were at Brigham Young most of the players were great, and some were characters. Occasionally, the phone would ring in the middle of the night, and my husband would be asked to go down to the square. One of the players would be sitting in the middle of the square screaming profanities about Joseph Smith and BYU. Wally would take him home and calm him down.

While we were with Brigham Young University in Yokohama at the Japan Bowl one of the BYU players, who later became famous, was sampling the local Imperial Sake. Wally was in a coach's meeting, and I went upstairs to collect my children who were in the players' rooms supposedly playing cards. At BYU no drinking or smoking is allowed. It's an excellent school with firm rules which some students don't follow. I arrived at the room to find the door open and a bathtub full of sake and beer. The players were obviously enjoying the refreshments. Interestingly, the next day these players played one of their greatest games.

When we were in Pittsburgh Terry Bradshaw was still playing. He was a terrific guy, really nice. He had some tough times. The people in Pittsburgh gave him grief, but he led the Steelers to four Super Bowls. One day he came out to our house. We were getting ready to move to Miami. He was looking for a house, and he wanted to see ours. Our son Andrew was just two weeks old. Terry asked if he could hold him. I have never seen hands as big as Terry Bradshaw's. He held our son easily in one hand. I was nervous and afraid that he might drop the baby. I forgot about all the footballs he had carried. But Terry told me that when he was a little boy his mother used to keep him home from school because he was the oldest. He took care of all the *youngins*. And he loved it! Terry was really a nice guy.

While Wally was coaching at the University of Pittsburg one of the high school players he recruited was Danny Marino. That spring when Danny graduated from high school we were invited to his graduation party. It was a great neighborhood party, big crowd, wonderful food. Danny was a super player at Central Catholic in

Pittsburgh, well-liked and supported by all his neighbors. Lots of schools were recruiting him. At the party I remember wondering how far this *home-town* kid would go. He certainly did go far! Danny was *the* quarterback for the Miami Dolphins. His picture appears on magazine covers. He does sports advertising and is a nationally known sports figure.

The New York Athletic Club had an award called the Hertz Number One Award. It was given to the outstanding senior all-around athlete in each state. My son Jon won this award for the state of Michigan. The presenter was O.J. Simpson. He gave an inspirational talk telling how he grew up and how he overcame adversity. He spoke to each awardee. When he met Jon he shook his hand and posed for a picture with Jon. O.J. had obviously done his homework about these players because he knew how many touchdown passes Jon had made and encouraged him to go forward in his career. His remarks were truly an inspiration. After the awards we ran into O.J. several times at the Pro Bowl and at the Super Bowl. He always had time to speak to us, and he always asked about Jon. It's sad and disappointing to see how his life has changed.

When Bob Brodhead was the athletic director at LSU we knew him well. Bob used to leave rocks on his car and tape on his doors to make sure nobody tinkered with anything, to be certain no bombs were planted, that no one sneaked into his room. The fans were so serious about football in Baton Rouge you didn't know what might happen. Bob was a skeptical person. If the rocks were moved on his car he didn't get into it. There was a coach at Tennessee who would find a moving truck parked in front of his house when the season wasn't going well. He was told someone had ordered it to come and pick up his furniture! Not a very subtle hint. **For Sale** signs turn up in coaches' yards. As you can see some folks take football very seriously. You laugh at the seriousness of it because you can't help but laugh. You've put your life in the hands of a group of eighteen year old kids, or *bigger kids--* the pros, on a playing field. The bottom line is if you don't win, you move or you're fired. Winning is everything!

At one time my husband hosted a football show on Sunday mornings. He would come home and go upstairs to relax before he had to go back to the office. One Sunday there was a knock at the door. We hadn't played the best game the night before. So when

I opened the door one of the big boosters was standing there. He wanted to know where Wally was, and when I explained he was soaking in the tub, this guy went past me, up the stairs, into the bathroom, and sat down on the edge of the tub. He proceeded to tell Wally what went wrong with the game. He was a big booster and gave lots of money to the school. So he seemed to feel he had every right!

When we were with the Detroit Lions Raymond Berry was the receiver coach, a super person. On road trips he would always say, "Eyes to the sky" because when the team would disembark from the buses at the hotel, there'd be a group of women waiting to catch a glimpse of the players. These women are known as *Football Groopies*. Berry would always tell the guys not to be distracted, not to look at them, "Game's the important thing. Eyes to the sky."

When we were at Kentucky one of the coaches was sent to spy on another team. He tried to get into their practice which is not allowed. So he climbed a telephone pole pretending to be a phone repairman. The team saw him, and they all turned around and pointed at him. Needless to say, he left.

When Florida State was number two in the nation Bobby

Bowden was the head coach. At that time Wally was the head coach at Tulane, his first head coaching job. Tulane was scheduled to play FSU that season which was sort of like sending David out to meet the giant. Tulane was a little scrub team, and Florida State was tops in the nation. I was invited to speak to the FSU women's booster club in Tallahassee. In my speech I praised the FSU football team as a great team. I closed my remarks with the hope that these Real Women would convince Bobby to go easy on Tulane and not beat us too badly. Well, it so happened that when Florida State came to New Orleans to play we beat them! It was the most exciting game Tulane played all season. Our son Jon threw three touchdown passes against them! People just went crazy. A couple of days later I received a note saying, "Please do not come back to speak to the women's booster club again. You put a jinx on us by telling us how good we were."

One time while we were at Virginia Tech we were going to play Alabama. At that time VT was leading the nation in passing with Don Strock as quarterback. It was one of their best seasons. Bear Bryant wrote an article describing VT as one of the best teams to play Alabama in a long time--how great they were, how tough it was going to be to beat them. Game day was cold and rainy. The Alabama team came out on the field in heavy, red parkas. They had heat fans running on the sidelines. Virginia Tech came out without warmups because they had expected it to be warm. They were shivering, trying to get ready to play. When they took the field to warm up Bear Bryant walked over wearing his famous houndstooth hat. He walked up and down in front of the VT bench without saying a word. He glared at the players and stood by the goal post continuing to glare throughout VT's warm-up time. We lost that game before it started. *The Bear* had intimidated the team, just this one man. He intimidated them so much it threw them off. That's part of the war games, confuse the enemy. The same thing happens when offensive and defensive lines face each other. Anything is fair game--Moms, wives and girl friends, virility. They're trying to win by intimidation before the play is even called. Well, Bear Bryant certainly won by intimidation. This game is so serious some coaches and players do win by intimidation.

There are states where dedication to football is positively over-whelming. For instance, an interesting thing about Nebraska football is that unless you are wearing something red you can't get in the stadium. Half the cars in the parking lot are red. You've never been to a football game until you hear all those Nebraska Cornhuskers screaming and yelling.

It's the same way at Arkansas. It was the Saturday of my first Arkansas football game. I went to the grocery store about 11:00 A.M. to buy food before the game. Everything was closed because everyone in the whole town had gone to the game. When Arkansas played Texas in Austin I called long distance to wish Wally and the Razorbacks good luck. The operator answered, "Hook 'em, Horns." I couldn't believe this long distance operator was already so into the spirit of Texas football she was actually answering like that. Texas is one of the biggest football states in the country. They take the game mighty seriously down there. The getups, the wild outfits, the face paint, the overturned cars. This is Texas football. They have more high school teams in Texas than several other states put together.

Rivalry between college football teams is a tradition as old as the game itself. The student bodies of each college try to out-yell, out-sing, out-perform each other at every opportunity. Some students get so hyped that they even try to steal the rival's mascot. They sneak on the opponent's campus and spray their school colors and team name and sometimes crude comments on walls, buildings, and sidewalks.

In the state of Florida the fans from the University of Florida and those from Florida State University wage highway wars. The fans from both schools living in the southern parts of the state have to travel Interstate 75 as far north as Gainesville where UF is located. On game weekends the road is bumper-to-bumper with vans, cars, RV's, trailers, buses. It is obvious which school each vehicle is headed toward. These fans mock each other from car-to-car as they pass. At times tempers flare and good judgment disappears, especially when a #1 ranking in the national polls is at stake. The drivers dart in-and-out, pass on the shoulder, or in the median, and all the passengers yell insults at each other and challenge each other waving their team banners and flags. This pre-game activity is almost as fierce as that which follows at the actual game.

The stadium at Notre Dame does not open until shortly before game time. Just before the gates open the Notre Dame Band begins to march and play through the campus. All the fans fall in behind the band and follow it to the stadium. It's like a modern-day Pied

Piper scene. And it's not difficult to understand just how intimi-
dating this awesome sight must be to the visiting team and fans.

The Louisiana State University mascot is a tiger. Mike travels
to the games in a large cage on wheels which has a microphone
wired into it. He is a magnificent creature. He has a full-time handler
who takes care of him and escorts him to games. At various times
during the game the handler drags a long stick across the bars of
Mike's cage. Mike responds with a ferocious growl which is amplified
by the microphone and broadcast over the PA system. Of course,
the LSU fans go wild! The thunderous roar from the stadium is
ear-splitting.

Texas A&M is the home of the Texas Aggies. The university is
well-known for its Twelfth Man tradition and its superb military-
style marching band of some 200-300 corps members. The A&M
Corps of Cadets stands throughout the entire game to assure the
team and coaches that each one of them is ready and willing to go
into the game if need be, the 12th man on the team. This tradition
is the result of an actual event that took place in the early 1920's
when the coach literally had no substitutes for injured players, and
a student suited up for play and stood on the sidelines in case he

was needed.

Stanford is another university whose marching band is incredible both in size and showmanship. Fans are quick to realize that the band does not wear uniforms. At times the band shows up in beach garb. Other times the dress for the day might be goggles, caps, anything goes with this innovative group in order to thrill the fans and TV audience.

The Arkansas Razorbacks yell *Sooooie Pig* throughout the game. The fight song for the Sooners of Oklahoma is quite rowdy. At Navy the midshipmen stand during the games to support the team. Nothing is quite as impressive as the Florida State University Seminole Indian Chief who enters the stadium bareback on his painted pony carrying a flaming spear down the middle of the field. He hurls the flaming spear into the ground in front of the visiting team declaring war. Talk about intimidation!

Coaches and teams believe that certain shirts, socks, shoes, ties, hats, or caps are their lucky talisman, and they insist on wearing this particular piece of clothing on every game day. Of course, it's presumed that the article of clothing has been washed between games. Fans are just as superstitious. When it comes to the game uniform itself, coaches, teams, and fans all know that the *home* jersey is always the one which guarantees a win!

There are unforgettable memories from our post-season experiences, too. When we were with the Dolphins Joe Robbie was the owner at that time, and we'd occasionally see him. Wally knew him, of course. He really didn't know me though we'd met a few times. We were at the Super Bowl at the Commissioner's party which is held on the Friday night before the Sunday game. This is a huge party, lots of good food and drinks freely flowing. There's an area roped off for celebrities. You need a special button to get in. Wally had one, but I didn't, so he went in and I watched from the outside. Gil Brandt who was in charge of player personnel with the Dallas Cowboys came along and asked about Wally. When I told him he was inside Gil gave me his button so I could go in, too. This was another case of someone I'd heard a lot of mean press about, who, at least at that time, was very thoughtful. Of course, Gil was so well known he really didn't need a button. He walked in behind me. We stayed quite late, and when we came out we saw Mr. Robbie wandering around in the parking lot. I got into the car. Wally went over to him. He'd had a bit too much to drink. So Wally offered to give him a ride back to his hotel which he accepted. I had already gotten into the back seat, so Mr. Robbie could ride up front. Wally opened the door. Mr. Robbie bent down to get in. He looked into the back seat, saw me sitting there, assumed I was a hooker, and said, "Now wait a minute, what's going on here?" We did take him to his hotel, and the next day he didn't remember anything.

There are many more stories I could tell you, but the season is about to begin.

ON WITH THE GAME!

Please send me your football stories! I'm hard at work on the game plan for my next book. I would love to hear how your families have been affected by this crazy game.

Real Women Know Football
5067 Fisherville Road
Simpsonville, KY 40067
pegenglish@aol.com

AROUND HIS OWN END

THE REAL WOMAN'S PLAYBOOK

TALK THE TALK
You're in the huddle now. If you want to call the plays you have to talk the talk. Football jargon is a language all its own. Understanding this language will increase your enjoyment of the game and make you the expert at the cocktail party. Perhaps this list of football **Talk, Strategies, Plays,** or **TSP,** will help. OK, quarterbacks go for it.

1ST & 10
First down with ten yards to go for another first down.

2ND & 7
Second down with seven yards to go for a first down.

3RD & 15
Third down with fifteen yards to go for a first down. This happens when a team looses yardage or gets a penalty.

AROUND HIS OWN END, OR END RUN
A runner carries the ball around the end of the line of scrimmage.

CLIPPING

BENCH WARMER
A player who practices all the time and sits on the bench during the game. He may never play a game but is a member of the team. He is the wallflower of the football world. He may go to the dance and never get to dance. Bear Bryant once said, "... they also are valuable to the team, who only sit and wait."

BIG HIT
A great block or tackle done with power. You can usually hear the groan of the player or the sound of the hit.

CHAIN
A metal chain that is ten yards long and is attached to two tall metal poles. The chain is used to measure distance for first downs.

CHAIN GANG
The people on the sidelines holding the chain. They can be iden-tified by their bright colored vests.

CLIPPING
Throwing the body across the back of the opponent's legs or hitting him from behind unless the opponent is a runner.

"Men have no concept of time."

COLLEGE DRAFT
This is held approximately the first week in April. The National Football League picks the outstanding college football players for their NFL teams. Each team has a pick in a series of drafts--first round draft choice, second round draft choice, continuing for six to eight rounds. The first and second round draft choices get the most money and usually a bonus for signing with a team.

DEFENSIVE TEAM
The team without the ball.

DELAY OF GAME
Play must resume within thirty seconds or a penalty is called.

DOWN
A down starts with the snap of the ball and ends when the whistle is blown. This is one full play. A team gets four downs to make ten yards.

EATING THE BALL

EATING THE BALL
The term used when the quarterback simply falls on the ball because he knows there is no other alternative.

ELIGIBLE RECEIVER
They are the players on the offensive team who can legally catch a pass--the two ends and the three backfield players. These guys aren't looking for dates. They are looking for the football.

END LINE
The line at the back of the end zone where the goal post stands.

END ZONE
The ten yard area between the goal line and the end line with the goal post.

FACE MASK
The face mask covers the face and is attached to the helmet. Thou shall not grab or hold the face mask, twist it or turn it. A player's head is inside.

FAIR CATCH
The only time this is allowed is in a kicking situation. The receiver raises his right hand to signal that he will not advance the ball when caught. The defensive team is not allowed to touch the receiver.

FIRST DOWN
The first of four opportunities given to the offensive team to gain ten yards.

FORWARD MOTION
The result of the offensive team's effort to move the ball forward and cross the line of scrimmage.

FUMBLE
The term used when the ball carrier loses possession of the ball. He drops the ball and it is not recovered.

GAME PLAN
A set of plans designed by the coaches for the players to use in the game

GOAL POST
The **Y**-shaped post placed on each end line at the back of the end zone. The uprights, as they are sometimes referred to, are eighteen feet, six inches apart and are attached to a crossbar ten feet high.

GRIDIRON
The football term for the playing field.

HAIL MARY
This is usually a last minute pass. It is thrown into the end zone with the hope that it will be caught by the receiver for a touch-down. It is called the HAIL MARY because there is only a prayer of a chance it will work.

HALF THE DISTANCE TO THE GOAL
The football is moved half the distance to the goal line.

"That's really cute guys...now can we try the I Formation."

HALFTIME
The fifteen minute period between the first half and second half.

HANGTIME
The time the ball is in the air after it has been kicked.

HASH MARKS
The set of short white lines that mark each yard on the field.

HUDDLE
The offensive team huddles behind the line of scrimmage in the middle of the field before a play. The quarterback tells the team what play is going to be called.

I-FORMATION
A formation where the two offensive backs line up behind the quarterback.

INELIGIBLE RECEIVER
No linemen are allowed down field before the pass is thrown. They would be ineligible to catch the ball. If one of them catches the ball, a penalty is called.

INTERCEPTION
A defensive player catches an offensive pass.

KICKOFF
A free kick to start the game, the second half, and after each score.

LINE OF SCRIMMAGE
The imaginary line eleven inches wide, the length of the football, which separates the offensive and defensive teams. The line of scrimmage moves anywhere on the field determined by the placement of the football.

MVP
The Most Valuable Player of the game.

NEUTRAL ZONE
The eleven inches separating the offensive and defensive teams--
the line of scrimmage.

OFFICIALS
They enforce the rules and should be considered neutral to both
teams. They are:
- B - Back Judge
- F - Field Judge
- L - Line Judge
- S - Side Judge
- H - Head Linesman
- U - Umpire
- R - Referee--The Boss

OVERTIME
A game cannot end in a tie for the Pro teams. If the game is tied,
another fifteen minutes of play is added to the game. If the game is
still tied after overtime, another fifteen minutes of play is added. If
there is still a tie after two overtime periods, the game goes into
SUDDEN DEATH. At this point the team who scores first wins
the game.

PASS INTERFERENCE
You cannot interfere with or impede the intended pass receiver. This is a penalty. After he catches the ball, he's fair game.

PENALTY MARKERS
The yellow flag thrown by the officials at the time of a penalty.

PERSONAL FOUL
Unnecessary roughness, clipping, piling on, kicking, or hitting with your fists are not allowed. This results in a penalty.

PILING ON
The term when players deliberately jump or fall on the ball carrier after the whistle has blown resulting in a pile. (Penalty)

PLAYBOOK
The book of plays designed by the coaches used to instruct the players.

POCKET
The formation used by the offensive line to protect the quarterback when he drops back to pass.

PUNT
One team kicks the ball to the other team. This is usually used on the fourth down when there is no possibility for a first down.

QUARTERS
There are four quarters in a football game. In pro football and college football each quarter consists of fifteen minutes playing time. These four quarters make up the sixty minutes allowed for game play. In high school the quarters are twelve minutes long.

SACK
The term used when the quarterback is knocked down while attempting a play.

SECONDARY
The players in the defensive backfield consisting of two cornerbacks, a STRONG safety, and a WEAK safety.

SNAP
The ball is snapped by the center when he passes the ball between his legs to the quarterback or kicker to begin the play.

STRONG SIDE
The side of the offensive formation with the most players.

SUDDEN DEATH
If either team has not scored in the Overtime period, the game goes into Sudden Death. There is no set period of time. The first team to score wins the game.

TIME OUT
Each team may call three time outs per half. The time outs last two minutes. A team calls a time out for several reasons--to distract the other team's concentration, to change a play, or if they are not ready for play and don't want a delay of game penalty. Strategy is involved in the use of time outs. Teams will use the time out calls when necessary.

TURF
The ground surface on which the game is played. This is either artificial grass or natural grass.

TURNOVER
A fumble or interception causing the possession of the ball to change hands between teams.

TWO MINUTE WARNING
A time out called by the Field Judge when there are two minutes left in the first half and only two minutes left in the game.

WEAK SIDE
The side of the offensive formation with the least amount of players.

X-Y-Z

Letters indicating certain players for written play formations. These letters aide coaches in teaching players from the chalkboard. The sports commentators utilize them when explaining plays to the TV viewers.

They are:

    X - Split End

    Y - Tight End

    Z - Flanker

The X's and the O's that you see on the TV instant replay represent the offense (O) and the defense (X).

STRATEGIES

AUDIBLE
A change of play by the quarterback at the line of scrimmage. If the defense is lined up in such a way that the original offensive play will not work the quarterback calls a new play.

BLITZING
A secondary player crosses the line of scrimmage the moment the ball is snapped in order to knock down the quarterback before he has time to throw the ball.

BLOCKED KICK
The defensive team blocks the offensive team's attempt to kick the ball.

COIN TOSS
Weather conditions, wind direction, and sun position affect a game and the plays that called. Coaches take all these things into consideration before the game. The captains are prepared to make the choice long before the toss of the coin. This is all part of the game plan.

FAKED INJURY
A player may pretend he is hurt in order to gain additional time for his team.

MAN-TO-MAN COVERAGE
A defensive player covering an offensive receiver one on one.

ON SIDES KICK
A short kickoff attempted by the kicking team in order to try to recover the ball and retain possession of it. The ball must travel ten yards.

OUT OF BOUNDS
A player carrying the ball may step out of bounds so the clock will stop giving more time to his team.

SHIFT
The offense moves to a different formation before the ball is snapped.

SHOTGUN
The quarterback uses this formation to give himself more time to throw the ball. He lines up about seven yards behind the center instead of right behind him. The center snaps the ball all the way back to the quarterback. It takes longer for the defensive team to get to the quarterback in this formation.

PLAYS

BOOTLEG
The quarterback fakes a handoff to the back then actually keeps the ball himself and turns in the opposite direction away from the back to fake the defensive team.

DRAW
This is a fake pass. It is a running play designed to look like a pass. The quarterback drops back to pass and then hands the ball off to a running back.

FORWARD PASS
The quarterback passes the ball downfield to a receiver.

HANDOFF
One offensive player hands the ball to another offensive player.

LATERAL
To pass the ball backward.

OPTION
The quarterback can choose to keep the ball and run or pass the ball to a back.

"Talk about a bad hair day!"

SWEEP
An end run with two lineman leading interference for the runner.

TRAP
A lineman pulls back from the line and deliberately allows the defensive lineman to penetrate the line. The offensive lineman then blocks the defender to the side.

THE END zone

Printed in the United States
23472LVS00001B/391-438